JB
813.54   Wheeler, Jill C.,
WHE   1964-
SNICKET
          Lemony Snicket.

D1404202

$21.35

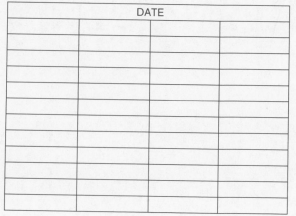

DATE			

Children's Authors

Lemony Snicket

Jill C. Wheeler
ABDO Publishing Company

visit us at
www.abdopublishing.com

Published by ABDO Publishing Company, 4940 Viking Drive, Edina, Minnesota 55435.
Copyright © 2007 by Abdo Consulting Group, Inc. International copyrights reserved in all
countries. No part of this book may be reproduced in any form without written permission from
the publisher. The Checkerboard Library™ is a trademark and logo of ABDO Publishing
Company.

Printed in the United States.

Cover Photo: Wesleyan University
Interior Photos: © Brett Helquist/HarperCollins p. 15; Corbis pp. 5, 7, 11, 13, 18, 23;
    © Meredith Heuer p. 16; Wesleyan University p. 9; Wire Image p. 17, 19, 20, 21

Series Coordinator: Megan Murphy
Editors: Megan M. Gunderson, Megan Murphy
Art Direction: Neil Klinepier

Library of Congress Cataloging-in-Publication Data

Wheeler, Jill C., 1964-
    Lemony Snicket / Jill C. Wheeler.
      p. cm. -- (Children's authors)
    Includes bibliographical references and index.
    ISBN-10 1-59679-767-3
    ISBN-13 978-1-59679-767-3
    1. Handler, Daniel--Juvenile literature. 2. Snicket, Lemony. Series of unfortunate events--
Juvenile literature. 3. Authors, American--20th century--Biography--Juvenile literature. 4.
Children's stories--Authorship--Juvenile literature. I. Title. II. Series.

    PS3558.A4636Z95 2006
    813'.54--dc22
                                                                    2005019537

Contents

Frighteningly Honest

Daniel Handler is not a fan of most children's books. He believes far too many of them are overly sweet and sappy. He also thinks many of them are unrealistic and misleading. He believes that children enjoy stories in which something scary or unfortunate occurs.

For Handler, bad is good. He is the author of the best-selling A Series of Unfortunate Events books. The first 11 titles in the series have sold more than 35 million copies. They are popular even though Handler warns his young readers not to read them. He tells children not to buy his books, or else to throw them off a mountain. But of course, they don't listen!

Growing up, Handler found that not every situation had a happy ending. He realized this when he saw bullies in his school go unpunished. And, he knew about world events such as the **Holocaust** at a young age. However, he was always able to find the humor in things. Handler's books combine his sense of humor with the understanding that bad things happen.

Handler is the first to admit his writing has succeeded beyond his wildest dreams. He says he never set out to write for children. Yet he finds it very satisfying. He says people never love a book the way they do when they are ten years old. So, Handler writes the kinds of books he wanted to read at that age.

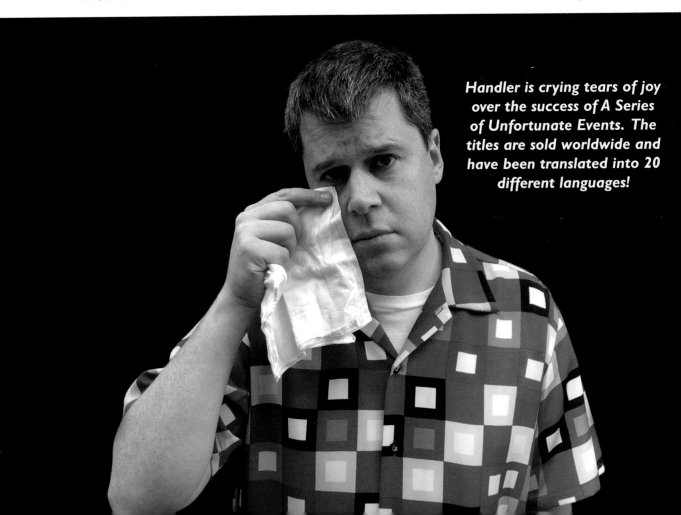

Handler is crying tears of joy over the success of A Series of Unfortunate Events. The titles are sold worldwide and have been translated into 20 different languages!

Not So Bad Beginning

Daniel Handler was born on February 28, 1970, in San Francisco, California. His father, Louis, was an accountant. His mother, Sandra, was a **dean** at City College of San Francisco. However, Sandra began her career as an opera singer. In fact, his parents met at the San Francisco Opera.

Daniel grew up in a quiet neighborhood. It was a long way from **Nazi** Germany, where his father had escaped as a young boy. At an early age, Daniel heard the dark and terrible stories of the **Holocaust**. For this reason, he was aware that bad things sometimes happen to children.

Daniel was an **avid** reader. He had many friends, but he preferred reading to playing kickball. His reading choices reflected his dark interests. Daniel had no time for fantasies or books about sports heroes. He preferred mysterious, creepy books. And he didn't like happy endings. His favorite authors were Roald Dahl and Edward Gorey.

Daniel grew up in San Francisco. He says his parents often left the phone unanswered while they were reading. Today, he carries on this tradition.

Daniel's own life was far from creepy. He played the piano, and later the accordion. He said he took up playing the accordion just to bother his parents. Daniel also liked investigating and collecting things. He was always hoping for a mystery to solve.

College in Connecticut

Daniel graduated from Lowell High School in San Francisco in 1988. After graduation, he traveled across the country to attend Wesleyan University in Middletown, Connecticut. There, he **majored** in both American studies and English.

Daniel began having some health problems in college. He would occasionally faint for no apparent reason. One day in English class, he collapsed into the lap of fellow student Lisa Brown. Daniel says he liked Lisa because she resembled Wednesday, the dark, gloomy daughter from *The Addams Family*. Soon, Daniel and Lisa started dating.

Daniel began writing poetry in college. In fact, his poetry won an **Academy of American Poets** prize in 1990. But when he noticed his poems kept getting longer, he changed to writing novels. Following his graduation from Wesleyan in 1992, Daniel was awarded an **Olin Fellowship** to write a novel.

The following year, Daniel and Lisa moved from Middletown to San Francisco. There, Daniel took whatever job he could get to pay the bills. He wrote comedy for a radio

show called the *House of Blues Radio Hour*. He also focused on his first adult novel, *The Basic Eight*. The story is set in a high school based on Daniel's own Lowell High School.

Daniel recalls that his dark sense of humor made him popular in school.

Unlikely Children's Author

Handler was nearly done writing *The Basic Eight* when he and Lisa moved to Manhattan, New York. By then, they were married. The couple moved so Lisa could study design at the Pratt Institute. Handler also hoped the move would help him find a publisher for his novel.

The Basic Eight was rejected 37 times. Finally in 1999, St. Martin's Press agreed to publish the book. **Critics** said *The Basic Eight* was pretty good. They praised Handler's way with words. Yet the book never became a best seller.

The Basic Eight helped Handler get noticed though. He wrote the story for adults, yet the characters are teenagers. This caused some people to ask Handler to consider writing for children. Then he met an editor named Susan Rich, who worked for HarperCollins. She suggested the same thing.

Handler had always believed bad things made for good stories. But, he thought his stories would not be appropriate for children because they were too dark. He wanted to prove he was the wrong type of person to write for children.

So as a joke, Handler told Rich of his book idea about three orphans and their mishaps. Handler thought she would realize he was joking. He was sure she would leave him alone after that. Instead, Rich loved the idea! And, she encouraged him to put his story down on paper.

Handler had agreed to make a movie based on the Baudelaire orphans before the first book was even published.

Introducing Lemony Snicket

Handler took Rich's advice. He turned his story idea into a children's series. He called it A Series of Unfortunate Events. It is about the three Baudelaire children, Violet, Klaus, and Sunny. In the first book, the children are orphaned and sent to live with their distant relative, the evil Count Olaf. Then one bad thing happens after another.

Handler signed a contract with HarperCollins for four books based on the Baudelaire orphans. The publisher released the first volume in 1999. It is titled *The Bad Beginning.* Brett Helquist added to the book's success by creating spooky illustrations for it.

Lemony Snicket **narrates** *The Bad Beginning*, as he does all the books in the series. Handler had created the name while researching *The Basic Eight*. As part of his research, he had contacted various organizations for information. However, he did not want them to have his real name. So, he made up the name Lemony Snicket.

The name grew more popular as time went on. Handler wrote letters to the editor under the name Lemony Snicket. He used the name to order pizzas, too. He thought it was a great **pseudonym**.

Handler often names his characters after prominent literary figures. He says he does this because he has such a difficult time coming up with character names. Handler named the main characters of his popular series after a famous French poet, Charles Baudelaire.

Surprising Success

As Lemony Snicket, Handler continued to write books about the Baudelaire orphans. The second volume in the series was also released in 1999. It is called *The Reptile Room*. Volume three, *The Wide Window*, and volume four, *The Miserable Mill*, followed in 2000.

Handler did not think A Series of Unfortunate Events would sell very well. He said he thought kids would like it. However, he did not think parents, teachers, and librarians would. He was prepared to see the books fail miserably.

To Handler's surprise, the series was anything but a failure. Young readers loved the books. Word spread from kid to kid and bookstore to bookstore. Lemony Snicket became a popular character, too.

Daniel and Lisa returned to San Francisco shortly after the first A Series of Unfortunate Events books were published. By then, Handler was already working on another adult novel, *Watch Your Mouth*. That book was published in 2000 under his real name.

A Series of Unfortunate Events was alarmingly successful. So, HarperCollins wanted Handler to write more books for the series. He signed on for a total of 13 books. But, he took a break in the middle of them to pen *Lemony Snicket: The Unauthorized Biography*. This book created even more mystery about who the author really was.

Handler likes his characters to use books to solve mysteries. Klaus Baudelaire in particular is known for applying things he has read to current "unfortunate" situations.

15

Mr. Snicket's Representative

Part of Handler's job as a successful author was to visit bookstores and schools to promote his books. He made appearances to sign copies of his books and talk to fans. There was just one problem though. His readers expected to

Lemony Snicket is rarely seen in public. The only pictures ever taken of him are from the back.

meet Lemony Snicket, not Daniel Handler.

However, Handler quickly came up with the perfect excuse. At each appearance, he made up a story about something terrible happening to Mr. Snicket. Some mishap always prevented the author from showing up. Handler came instead as Lemony Snicket's "representative."

Of course the fans always knew what was going on. Yet they came anyway to hear Mr. Snicket's representative discuss the latest book. Many even showed up dressed as orphans.

Handler appreciates the fan support. He receives thousands of letters and e-mails from his young followers. And, he replies to them as Lemony Snicket. He assures them that if there is anything they can do to help the Baudelaire orphans, he will let them know.

Handler often plays the accordion during his appearances at bookstores and schools. In fact, the author has always had a gift for drama. Playing Lemony Snicket is just one more role for Handler.

Movie Time

In 2002, people began talking seriously about making a movie based on A Series of Unfortunate Events. Handler signed on with Paramount Pictures to write the **screenplay** for the film. At first, it was expected to be a small production.

The project had its own unfortunate events. Both the movie's **producer** and director left because of budget problems. Finally, the movie began to take shape in fall 2003.

Meanwhile, Daniel and Lisa had several new developments of their own. They moved into a restored Victorian home in San Francisco. It looks much like Count Olaf's mansion. And their son, Otto, was born around the same time production began on the movie.

Jim Carrey

In total, Handler wrote eight **drafts** of the screenplay. Eventually, the movie studio chose another writer to compose the final script. The budget also increased dramatically to about $140 million. Jim Carrey took on the role of the evil Count Olaf.

Lemony Snicket's A Series of Unfortunate Events was released in December 2004. The movie took in $30 million at the **box office** the first weekend it was released.

Handler with Meryl Streep (left) and Emily Browning (right) at the Los Angeles premiere of **Lemony Snicket's A Series of Unfortunate Events**

Man of Many Talents

Handler's advice for anyone who wants to be a writer is to always carry a notebook.

Handler continues to work on new titles for A Series of Unfortunate Events. He used to write three volumes each year. Now he writes just one per year.

Handler treats writing like a regular job. He works from morning until early afternoon each day. In the evenings, he enjoys spending time with Otto, cooking, and watching videos with Lisa. In addition to writing books for children and adults, Handler has contributed articles to several magazine publications, including *Newsday*. And, he wrote a **screenplay** for the independent film *Rick* in 2004.

Handler likes to experiment with music, too. He plays the accordion in a band. One of the band members writes a theme song for each audiobook **version** of A Series of Unfortunate Events. Handler plays the accordion for these recordings, too.

The twelfth book of the Lemony Snicket series came out in fall 2005. Most recently, Handler was working on another novel for adults. He said it is about pirates. He also hopes to create a movie musical. Regardless of the project, it will be a fortunate event for Handler's many fans.

*Handler's Very Fervent Devotees (VFD). The letters **VFD** first appeared in volume five, **The Austere Academy**. They have stood for many things since then. In this instance, fervent means enthusiastic or excited. And, a devotee is someone who is a huge fan.*

Glossary

Academy of American Poets - a national organization devoted to the art of poetry.

avid - enthusiastic or eager.

box office - income from ticket sales of a movie or play. Also, a booth or office where tickets for a movie or play are sold.

critic - a professional who gives his or her opinion on art, literature, or performances.

dean - a person at a university who is in charge of guiding students.

draft - an early version or outline.

Holocaust - the killing of 6 million Jewish people, as well as many other prisoners, by Nazi forces during World War II.

major - to focus on a particular subject or field of study in college.

narrate - to tell a story. A person who narrates is a narrator.

Nazi - a member of the German political party that controlled Germany under Adolf Hitler.

Olin Fellowship - money awarded to a college student to support his or her research or creative writing outside of the classroom.

producer - a person who supervises or provides money for a play, television show, movie, or album.

pseudonym (SOO-duh-nihm) - a fictitious name, often used by an author.

screenplay - the script for a movie.

script - the text or words that actors say in a television show or a movie.

version - a different form or type from the original.

Web Sites

To learn more about Lemony Snicket, visit ABDO Publishing Company on the World Wide Web at **www.abdopublishing.com**. Web sites about Lemony Snicket and Daniel Handler are featured on our Book Links page. These links are routinely monitored and updated to provide the most current information available.

A Series of Unfortunate Events is popular all over the world. The books have been translated and sold in many foreign countries, including Iran.

Index